Duck Hunting

By Randy Frahm

Consultant:
Paul Beinke
President
Lakes Region Chapter
Minnesota Waterfowl Association

CAPSTONE
HIGH-INTEREST
BOOKS

an imprint of Capstone Press
Mankato, Minnesota

Capstone High-Interest Books are published by Capstone Press
151 Good Counsel Drive, P.O. Box 669, Mankato, Minnesota 56002
http://www.capstone-press.com

Library of Congress Cataloging-in-Publication Data
Frahm, Randy.
    Duck hunting/by Randy Frahm.
    p. cm.—(The great outdoors)
    Includes bibliographical references (p. 45) and index.
    ISBN 0-7368-0913-9
    1. Duck shooting—Juvenile literature. [1. Duck shooting. 2. Hunting.] I. Title.
II. Series.
SK333.D8 F73 2002
799.2'44—dc21   2001000092

Summary: Describes the equipment, skills, conservation issues, and safety concerns of duck hunting.

Editorial Credits
Carrie A. Braulick, editor; Lois Wallentine, product planning editor; Timothy Halldin,
    cover designer and illustrator; Katy Kudela, photo researcher

Photo Credits
Capstone Press/Gary Sundermeyer, cover (bottom left), 4, 8 (foreground), 10, 14,
    22, 26, 35
Comstock, Inc., 1, 8 (background), 20 (background)
Gene Boaz, 17
Gregg R. Andersen, cover (bottom right), 12, 20 (foreground)
Mark Raycroft, 29 (all)
Photri-Microstock/Leonard Lee Rue, 32; Louie Bunde, 36
Rob and Ann Simpson, 7
Root Resources/Jim Flynn, 41 (top)
TOM STACK & ASSOCIATES/Barbara Gerlach, 40 (bottom)
Unicorn Stock Photos/Chris Brown, 30
Visuals Unlimited/Hank Andrews, 24; Cheryl A. Ertelt, 40 (top); Beth Davidow,
    41 (bottom); Gary C. Will, 42 (top); Hal Beral, 42 (bottom); Ron Spomer, 44
William H. Mullins, cover (top right), 19

1 2 3 4 5 6 07 06 05 04 03 02

Table of Contents

CHAPTER 1

Duck Hunting

Duck hunting is one of the most popular forms of hunting. Ducks are common throughout North America. They live on marshes, rivers, lakes, and oceans.

Most people hunt ducks for food and recreation. They may duck hunt to enjoy the outdoors or to spend time with friends and family. Many duck hunters enjoy the challenge of shooting at moving targets.

History of Duck Hunting

During the 1600s and 1700s, American Indians and early North American settlers hunted ducks. They ate the birds' meat and decorated their clothing with duck feathers. Market hunters sold duck meat and feathers for profit. These hunters shot ducks year-round. They killed as many ducks as they could.

Many duck hunters hunt for food and recreation.

By the late 1800s, people realized market hunters were killing too many ducks. By 1900, market hunting became illegal in North America.

Today, few duck hunters hunt for profit. Duck hunters usually hunt for recreation. They follow rules to maintain healthy duck populations.

Puddle Ducks

Two types of ducks live throughout North America. These types are puddle ducks and diving ducks.

Puddle ducks are the most commonly hunted North American ducks. These ducks live on small bodies of water such as ponds and marshes. These places are the ducks' habitats. The small water areas provide natural living conditions for the ducks.

Puddle ducks often eat aquatic plants. These plants grow in the water. They also eat field crops such as wheat and soybeans. Puddle ducks' legs are located near the center of their bodies. This placement helps the ducks walk on land to eat field crops.

Puddle ducks have legs located at the center of their bodies to help them walk on land.

Several puddle duck species live in North America. Animals in a species share certain physical features. North American puddle duck species include mallards, wood ducks, and blue- and green-winged teals.

Diving Ducks

North American duck hunters hunt diving duck species such as canvasbacks, redheads, goldeneyes,

Orange Duck

Ingredients:
4 duck breasts
1 quart orange juice
1 cup diced onions
1 cup diced carrots
2 crushed garlic cloves
1 teaspoon pepper
1/4 teaspoon nutmeg
1/4 teaspoon thyme leaves

Equipment:
Slow cooker

1. Place duck breasts in slow cooker.

2. Add all other ingredients to slow cooker.

3. Cover slow cooker and simmer for 6 hours at 250 degrees Fahrenheit (120 degrees Celsius) or until duck breasts are tender.

Serves: 4   *Children should have adult supervision.*

and ringneck ducks. Diving ducks usually have habitats on large bodies of water such as rivers, lakes, and oceans. Many diving ducks live on the Atlantic and Pacific Oceans.

Diving ducks dive and swim to locate food. Diving ducks mainly eat small fish. But some of these ducks feed heavily on plants that grow in the water.

Migration

Most ducks migrate each year during the fall. Ducks move from place to place when they migrate. Ducks migrate to escape the cold winter weather and to find food. Many ducks hatched in Canada fly to Mexico. Mexico has a much warmer climate than Canada and most of the United States. Each spring, the ducks fly from Mexico back to Canada to nest. These ducks then lay eggs and raise their young. Ducks usually follow natural features such as seacoasts or rivers as they migrate.

Ducks are strong, fast flyers. They fly between 35 and 50 miles (56 and 80 kilometers) per hour as they migrate. Migrating ducks can travel 1,000 to 1,500 miles (1,600 to 2,400 kilometers) in a few days.

CHAPTER 2

Equipment

Duck hunters use a great deal of equipment. They need a shotgun and shells. Many hunters use decoys and duck calls to attract ducks within shooting range. Duck hunters often use boats and blinds.

Shotguns

Hunters use shotguns to shoot ducks. Shotguns hold cases called shells. Shotgun shells contain small pellets called shot. A plastic or fiber container called a wad holds the pellets. Gun powder inside a shell creates an explosive charge when hunters fire a shotgun. The charge pushes the wad out of the gun's barrel. This long, metal tube is at the front of the gun. The pellets then spread out in the air. Ducks fall if enough pellets hit them.

Duck hunters use a variety of equipment as they hunt.

Shotgun

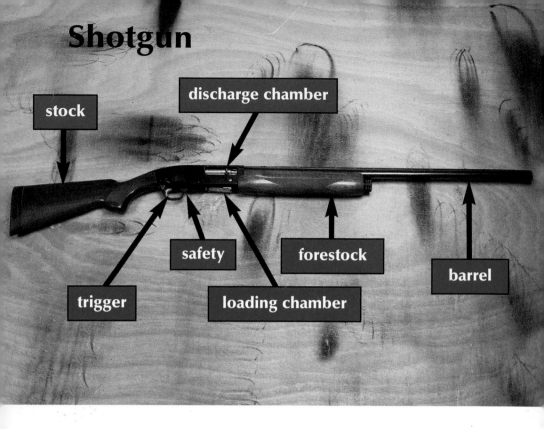

stock

discharge chamber

safety

forestock

barrel

trigger

loading chamber

Duck hunters use various types of shotguns. Most duck hunters use double-barrel, pump, or semi-automatic shotguns.

Double-barrel shotguns have two barrels. Some double-barrel guns have barrels located side by side. Other double-barrels have one barrel on top of another. Hunters must place another shell in a double-barrel's chamber after firing. This space holds the shells. The chamber is located in front of a lever called the trigger. Hunters pull the trigger back to fire a shotgun.

Pump and semi-automatic shotguns work differently from double-barrels. Hunters can shoot a pump shotgun once. They then must reload the gun by moving the gun's forestock back and forth. This part is located underneath the back end of a shotgun's barrel.

A semi-automatic shotgun is gas-operated. The explosive charge of a shell produces gas. The gas pushes the used shell out of the chamber. The gas also pushes a new shell into the chamber.

Duck hunters can buy shotguns with different gauges. A gun's gauge is the inside width of the barrel. Most shotgun gauges are measured in millimeters. Guns with low gauges are more powerful than guns with high gauges. Many duck hunters use 10- or 12- gauge shotguns. But some duck hunters use guns with gauges of 20 or more.

Shells

Shells have a hard outer coating. This coating usually is made of plastic. The shell's bottom is covered with metal. Duck hunting shells usually are about 3 inches (7.6 centimeters) long.

Shotgun shells have plastic outer coatings and metal bottoms.

Duck hunters use non-toxic shells. These shells contain pellets made of metals such as steel, iron, or tin. In the past, duck hunters used shells with lead pellets. But these pellets are poisonous. Many puddle ducks in heavily hunted areas died after they accidentally ate lead pellets. Today, it is illegal to hunt ducks with lead pellets in North America.

The shot inside of shells comes in different sizes. Most duck hunters use shot sizes from 1 to 5. Shells with No. 1 shot contain large pellets. Shells with No. 5 shot contain smaller pellets. Large shot travels farther than small shot. But shells with large shot contain fewer pellets than shells with small shot.

Shells have different shot weights and strengths of powder. This combination is called load. Loads can be field, standard, or magnum. Field loads contain the most lightweight shot. They also have the least powder charge. Standard loads contain heavier shot and have more powder charge than field loads. Guns that have more powder charge produce more power.

Magnum loads contain the heaviest shot and have the greatest powder charge. These loads also spray pellets in a closer pattern than field or standard loads.

Decoys

Ducks often land to join other ducks. Hunters place decoys to attract ducks to their hunting areas. These manufactured ducks are made of wood, plastic, or rubber. Duck hunters usually place them in the water. Weights tied to the decoys with heavy strings prevent them from floating away. Hunters may place some decoys on land.

Decoys are made to resemble the different duck species. They may look like mallards, teals, or canvasbacks. The type of decoy hunters use depends on the species they are hunting. Ducks are more likely to land near other members of the same species.

Boats

Duck hunters often use boats. Boats can carry hunters and equipment to ideal hunting locations.

Duck hunters use a variety of boats. They may use canoes on ponds, rivers, and marshes. Duck hunters often use jonboats. Jonboats have a square bottom. The square bottom helps hunters stand and shoot without tipping the boat over. Many duck hunters use pirogues. These boats have pointed ends and a wide bottom. Pirogues are stable and easy to move in shallow areas. Large motorboats allow hunters to move quickly in large lakes and oceans.

Duck hunters build blinds that blend into the surroundings to hide from ducks.

Hunters try to hide their boats from ducks. They often paint their boats to blend in with the surroundings. Hunters often slide their boats between tall plants.

Blinds

Many duck hunters use natural features such as hills, rocks, grass, or weeds to hide from ducks. But they often use their own hidden shelters. These shelters are called blinds. Some duck hunters purchase blinds from outdoor or sporting goods stores. Other duck hunters create blinds.

Duck hunters can create blinds in various ways. They may attach weeds or corn stalks to wire. In coastal areas, duck hunters may use rocks or driftwood along the shore. Some duck hunters use strips of a coarse woven fabric called burlap. They attach the strips to metal netting. Burlap can protect hunters from wind and help keep them warm. Many duck hunters attach blinds to boats or rafts. Hunters hide in or behind blinds until ducks are close enough to shoot.

Other Equipment

Other equipment is helpful to duck hunters. Hunters often use duck calls. Hunters blow into these small plastic or wooden tubes to attract ducks. The air flowing through the calls makes sounds similar to the sounds of certain duck species. Duck hunters use calls designed for the species that they want to shoot. Duck hunters often attach their calls to strings called lanyards. They then wear the lanyards around their neck.

Flashlights help hunters see in the dark. Ducks are most active near sunrise and sunset. Hunters

Duck hunters often wear chest waders to keep them dry in the water.

often travel to or leave their hunting locations in the dark. They usually carry waterproof flashlights that float.

Duck hunters carry other items. Some hunters carry a wing chart. This chart helps duck hunters identify the ducks they see. Duck hunters also may use binoculars. This viewing instrument helps duck hunters spot ducks from a distance.

Equipment

- Shotgun
- Shells
- Blind
- Boat
- Decoys
- Calls
- Waders
- Binoculars
- Wing chart
- Flashlight
- First aid kit
- Life jacket

Clothing

Duck hunters wear waterproof clothing. They often must walk through the water. Duck hunters wear waders to keep themselves dry. Waders are made of waterproof materials such as rubber and nylon. They may be hip boots or chest waders.

Hip boots are waterproof pants attached to boots. They cover a hunter's legs and have straps that connect to a hunter's belt.

Chest waders cover a hunter's legs and upper body. They usually have straps that fit over the shoulders. Chest waders often have boots attached to them.

Duck hunters often dress in layers. They then can add or remove clothes to stay comfortable. Many duck hunters wear nylon wind- and water-resistant jackets. Some duck hunters bring waterproof coats to protect them from rain. Duck hunters wear heavy coats, hats, and mittens or gloves in cold weather.

Most hunters wear camouflage clothing to hide from ducks. The colors of this clothing blend into the surroundings. Many hunters believe ducks are frightened by bright colors.

CHAPTER 3

Skills and Techniques

Duck hunters must learn to shoot properly. They may practice shooting at saucer-shaped practice targets called clay pigeons.

Some hunters practice calling. Each duck species makes a different type of sound. Duck hunters practice making realistic calls. Some of these duck hunters compete at the National Duck Calling Contest held each year in Stuttgart, Arkansas.

Jump Shooting

Some hunters sneak up on ducks to shoot at them. This practice is called jump shooting. Duck hunters usually jump shoot while they hunt puddle ducks. These ducks often rest on small bodies of water. It is easy for duck

Duck hunters may shoot ducks from blinds attached to boats.

Duck hunters often use calls to attract ducks.

hunters to sneak up on ducks in these
small areas.

Duck hunters who jump shoot may use
binoculars to look for ducks. They then
carefully approach the ducks that they see.
Hunters can hide behind trees, hills, tall
bushes, or weeds. The hunters come out of
hiding when they are close enough to shoot.
They then scare the birds into the air and
shoot at them.

Attracting Ducks

Duck hunters often use calls and decoys to attract ducks. Puddle duck hunters may use calls more often than diving duck hunters do. Decoys sometimes attract diving ducks without calls.

The amount of decoys duck hunters place in the water depends on the area's size. Duck hunters may place hundreds of decoys on large bodies of water. They may use only a few on small bodies of water.

Duck hunters place decoys in front of them. Some of the decoys should be within shooting range. Most duck hunters place decoys less than 20 to 30 feet (6 to 9.1 meters) away from them.

Hunters sometimes leave one side of a decoy arrangement open. Ducks often land in open areas.

Duck hunters should consider wind conditions when they place decoys. Ducks normally fly into the wind as they land. They spread their wings before landing. The wind blowing against their wings slows down the ducks and helps them

Duck hunters should have good shooting techniques to hit moving targets.

land. Hunters should face open areas of their decoy arrangements into the wind.

Duck hunters can place decoys in various arrangements. Duck hunters often place decoys in a long "J" shape. The bottom of the "J" is closest to the hunters. Ducks will often try to land in the curved, open bottom of the "J."

Puddle duck hunters sometimes place decoys in two groups on either side of their location. Ducks then may try to land between the two groups.

Puddle duck hunters also may place decoys in a "C" shape. Hunters place decoys in this shape on one side of their location. They try to face the "C's" opening into the wind.

Diving duck hunters often place long strings of decoys in the water. They may put the decoys in a "V" shape. Diving ducks often follow the path of decoys and try to land in the "V's" middle.

Shooting

Duck hunters must have good shooting technique to hit moving targets. They often need to adjust their angle of shooting. They must consider the ducks' flight speed and make sure they are within shooting range. They compare the length of the duck to the barrel width of the shotgun. The barrel should cover less than half of the duck.

Duck hunters often use the swing-through technique. A hunter holds a gun with one hand behind the trigger and the other hand under the gun's forestock. The hand underneath the forestock raises the barrel while the other hand brings the end of the gun to the shoulder. Hunters start their swing with the barrel behind the moving duck. They then swing the gun ahead of the duck in its flight path. The distance hunters leave between the duck and the barrel depends upon how fast the duck is moving, its angle, and the shooting range. The hunters then fire the gun in front of the bird. They keep moving the gun along the duck's line of flight after firing the gun.

Hunting Dogs

Duck hunters often use dogs to find and bring back ducks that are shot down. Dogs often find wounded ducks that otherwise might escape from hunters.

Hunting dogs must be properly trained. They must know how to sit, stay in one place, retrieve, and come when called. The dogs also need to sit quietly in a boat or blind.

Duck Hunting Dog Breeds

Labrador Retrievers

Labrador retrievers originally came from Canada. Many people call labradors "labs." Most labs are 21 to 24 inches (53 to 61 centimeters) tall. Labradors are muscular dogs with short, smooth coats. Labs can be black, yellow, or brown. The brown coloring is called chocolate. Most labs are solid in color. But some labs have a white marking on their chest. Labradors have oily coats that shed water. They are good swimmers.

Chesapeake Bays

Chesapeake Bays originally came from areas surrounding Chesapeake Bay on the eastern coast of the United States. This long, narrow body of water borders Maryland and Virginia. Chesapeake Bays usually are 21 to 26 inches (53 to 66 centimeters) tall. They can be various shades of tan or brown. The dogs may have a white spot on their chest, stomach, or paws. Chesapeake Bays have a double coat. The inner layer is dense and long. The outer coat is short and smooth. Chesapeake Bays sometimes have wavy hair on their shoulders, neck, and back. These dogs work especially well in cold, icy conditions.

Golden Retrievers

Golden retrievers originally came from England and Scotland. These dogs usually are 20 to 24 inches (51 to 61 centimeters) tall. They have thick coats. Golden retrievers' coats can be one of several shades. The color may vary from light tan to gold-red. All golden retrievers are solid in color. They are good swimmers.

CHAPTER 4

Conservation

Responsible duck hunters practice good conservation habits. They take care of duck habitats. Some duck hunters join clubs and donate money to protect duck habitats.

Wetlands

Wetlands provide ducks with a place to nest. These areas of shallow water have many plants. Wetlands are located along rivers, near lakes, in coastal areas, and in large areas of grass called prairies. Ducks use the plants to hide their nests from predators such as foxes, raccoons, and coyotes. These animals eat duck eggs.

One of North America's largest wetlands is the prairie pothole region. People sometimes call this area "North America's duck factory."

Duck hunters often hunt in wetland areas.

Some people help maintain areas and structures where ducks nest.

The prairie pothole region begins in the Canadian provinces of Alberta, Saskatchewan, and Manitoba. The region then extends south through the states of North Dakota, South Dakota, and Minnesota. The prairie pothole region is about 1,000 miles (1,600 kilometers) long and 300 miles (480 kilometers) wide.

Protecting Wetlands

Many activities can harm or ruin wetlands. Farmers may drain the water from wetlands to use the land to grow crops. People also drain wetlands to build roads, homes, and office buildings. The United States lost more than 4 million acres (1.6 million hectares) of wetlands between 1975 and 1995.

Federal, state, and provincial governmental agencies purchase some wetlands to provide ducks with habitats. These agencies may include the U.S. Fish and Wildlife Service and the Canadian Wildlife Service. Some wetlands owned by governmental agencies are refuges. Duck hunting is limited or illegal in these areas.

Governmental agencies also create programs to protect and restore wetlands. These programs may clean polluted water areas or maintain structures where ducks nest.

Some duck hunters join organizations that protect duck habitats. In 1937, hunters formed Ducks Unlimited (DU). Since then,

DU has preserved nearly 25 million acres
(10 million hectares) of duck habitat in
North America.

Regulations

Governmental agencies in North America
establish regulations to protect duck populations.
The rules prevent too many ducks from being
killed. The U.S. Fish and Wildlife Service
establishes federal duck hunting regulations
in the United States. This agency sometimes
suggests regulations to state governments.
But state governments establish most duck
hunting regulations.

The Canadian Wildlife Service works with
Canadian provinces to establish most regulations
in Canada. But provinces also create additional
hunting rules.

Governmental agencies also set limits on
the number of ducks hunters can kill in one day.
This number is called the daily bag limit.

North America also has duck hunting seasons.
Hunters can only hunt between these dates in the
fall. The season's length depends on the area's
duck population. Southern states start their

Duck hunters can hunt only during established hunting seasons.

seasons later in the fall than northern states do. Ducks usually do not migrate through southern states until late fall.

Governmental agencies also set rules for youth duck hunting. Youth hunters usually must pass a gun safety class and hunt with an adult. Young hunters sometimes can hunt without a license. But hunters age 16 and older usually need a license. These hunters also usually need to purchase federal permits or stamps.

Safety

Safety should be important to duck hunters. Some hunters take gun safety classes. Hunters should be aware of the weather conditions and their surroundings.

Gun Safety

Duck hunters should follow guidelines to make sure no one is accidentally shot. They should always store guns unloaded. They should never point a gun at another person or anything that they do not want to shoot. Duck hunters should make sure they can see the target clearly before they shoot at it.

Duck hunters should put a gun's safety on when they are not using it. This device located near the trigger prevents a gun from firing.

Duck hunters must be careful with their guns.

Other Safety Concerns

Other safety guidelines are important to duck hunters. Hunters in boats should wear life jackets. Duck hunters should hunt with another person. If one hunter is injured, the other can help.

Duck hunters should watch weather conditions. They should listen to the day's weather report before they go hunting. Duck hunters should stop hunting if a snowstorm occurs. Heavy snow can make it hard for hunters to see. Hunters then may become lost.

First Aid

Duck hunters should carry first aid kits in case they become injured. Items in first aid kits usually include scissors, gloves, medicine tape, and bandages. The kits also have gauze to cover wounds. Most kits have antibiotic ointment to protect wounds from germs.

Safe duck hunters are prepared for accidents. They know basic first aid skills and are careful with their guns. They know that being responsible can help them enjoy their sport.

Gun Safety

1. Treat all guns as if they were loaded.

2. Do not point a gun at anything you do not intend to shoot.

3. Make sure to identify the target before shooting. You should have a clear view of the target.

4. Keep your finger straight and off the trigger until you want to shoot.

5. Always control the direction of the barrel. Never point it toward other people.

6. Keep the safety on unless you want to shoot.

7. Keep the gun unloaded when you are not using it. Unload a gun immediately after you are finished using it.

8. Keep different shells separate from each other.

9. Do not shoot at hard surfaces. The bullets or pellets could bounce off these surfaces and injure someone.

10. Always check to see what is beyond your target. Bullets or pellets that miss the target may hit an object, person, or animal beyond the target.

11. Make sure the barrel is clear after a fall. A barrel that is blocked by an object may burst.

12. Do not lean a gun anywhere where it may slip and fall.

Mallard

Mallards are the most commonly hunted North American ducks. Mallards nest in Canada and the northern United States. Mallards that nest in Canada often spend winters in the southern United States and Mexico. Ducks that nest in the northern United States often do not migrate.

Description: Mallards are puddle ducks. Male mallards have a dark green head and a white band around their neck. They have a brown chest and a white underside. Female mallards are mostly brown with black spots. Mallards usually are 18 to 28 inches (46 to 71 centimeters) long. They weigh between 1.5 and 4 pounds (.7 and 1.8 kilograms).

Habitat: marshes, swamps, ponds, lakes, bays

Food: aquatic plants, seeds, insects, corn, wheat, soybeans

Wood Duck

Wood ducks nest throughout most of North America. They mainly nest in the eastern United States. Wood ducks spend winters in Mexico, southern California, and southeastern states such as Florida and Georgia. Wood ducks may live in the southern United States year-round.

Description: Wood ducks are puddle ducks. Male wood ducks have a bright green head. The head has a dark blue or black mask with white streaks. Male wood ducks also have a dull red chest, a green back, and a bright orange bill. Female wood ducks have a tan underside and a dark brown back. Their bill is gray with a black tip. Wood ducks are 15 to 21 inches (38 to 53 centimeters) long. They weigh between 1 and 2 pounds (.5 and .9 kilogram).

Habitat: swamps, ponds, rivers

Food: aquatic plants, acorns, corn, soybeans

Green-Winged Teal

Green-winged teals nest throughout most of Canada and the northern United States. They spend winters in the southern United States and Mexico.

Description: Green-winged teals are the smallest of all puddle ducks. They have dark green spots on their wings. Males have a dark green mask across their orange face. Their chest is tan with black spots. Females are tan with black spots. They have a dark brown streak across their eyes. Green-winged teals are 13 to 15 inches (33 to 38 centimeters) long and weigh between .5 and 1 pound (.2 and .5 kilogram).

Habitat: marshes, shallow lakes, ponds

Food: seeds, small aquatic animals, insects, corn, soybeans

Canvasback

Canvasbacks nest from central Alaska to western Canada. They also nest in the northern United States. Canvasbacks spend winters along the coasts of the Atlantic and Pacific Oceans and in Mexico.

Description: Canvasbacks are one of the largest diving ducks. They have a black bill and gray feet. Males have a dark orange or red head. They have a white body and a black chest. Females are brown with tan spots. Canvasbacks are 22 to 28 inches (56 to 71 centimeters) long. They weigh between 2 and 3 pounds (.9 and 1.4 kilograms).

Habitat: lakes, ponds, marshes, bays

Food: small fish, aquatic plants

Common Goldeneye

Common goldeneyes nest throughout Canada and the northern United States. They spend winters along the Pacific Ocean's coast and in the southern United States. They usually do not fly as far south for the winter as other ducks.

Description: Some people call common goldeneyes "whistlers." These diving ducks make a whistling sound as they fly. Common goldeneyes have a white throat and underside. Males have a black head, bill, back, and tail. They have a white spot behind their bill. Females have a brown head with no spot. Their sides are gray. Common goldeneyes are about 16 to 20 inches (41 to 51 centimeters) long. They weigh between 1.5 and 3.5 pounds (.7 and 1.6 kilograms).

Habitat: shallow lakes and ponds, shallow bays along sea coasts

Food: small fish, aquatic plants

Lesser Scaup

Lesser scaup nest in western Canada, Alaska, and the prairie pothole region. They spend winters in Mexico and along the coasts of the Atlantic and Pacific Oceans.

Description: Lesser scaup are diving ducks. They have gray-black wings with white edges and a blue-gray bill. Some people call them "bluebills." Males have a black head, neck, and tail. Their head may be light purple during fall and winter. They have a white underside and a gray back. Females are dark brown. They have a cream underside and a white ring behind their bill. Lesser scaup are 15 to 18 inches (38 to 46 centimeters) long and weigh between 1 and 2.5 pounds (.5 and 1.1 kilograms).

Habitat: marshes, ponds

Food: snails, small fish, seeds, aquatic plants

Words to Know

barrel (BA-ruhl)—the long, tube-shaped metal part of a gun that the bullet or pellets travel through

blind (BLINDE)—a hidden place from which duck hunters shoot ducks

camouflage (KAM-uh-flahzh)—coloring or covering that makes people look like their surroundings

gauge (GAYJ)—the measurement of the inside width of a gun's barrel

limit (LIM-it)—the number of ducks a hunter can kill and take home in one day

marsh (MARSH)—an area of wet, low land

migrate (MYE-grate)—to move from one place to another as the seasons change

safety (SAYF-tee)—a device that prevents a gun from firing

shot (SHOT)—lead or steel pellets in a shell

To Learn More

Bourne, Wade. *Decoys and Proven Methods for Using Them.* Memphis, Tenn.: Ducks Unlimited, 2000.

Livingston, A. D. *Duck and Goose Cookbook.* Mechanicsburg, Pa.: Stackpole Books, 1997.

Walton, Richard K. *North American Waterfowl.* National Audubon Society Pocket Guides. New York: A. A. Knopf, 1994.

Wilcox, Charlotte. *The Labrador Retriever.* Learning about Dogs. Mankato, Minn.: Capstone High-Interest Books, 1996.

Useful Addresses

Canadian Wildlife Service
Environment Canada
Ottawa, ON K1A 0H3
Canada

Ducks Unlimited
One Waterfowl Way
Memphis, TN 38120

Minnesota Waterfowl Association
3815 East 80th Street
Bloomington, MN 55425

National Bird Dog Museum
P.O. Box 774
Grand Junction, TN 38039

U.S. Fish and Wildlife Service
4401 North Fairfax Drive
Arlington, VA 22203

Internet Sites

Canadian Wildlife Service
http://www.cws-scf.ec.gc.ca/cwshom_e.html

Clay Pigeon Shooting Association
http://www.cpsa.co.uk

Ducks of the World
http://www.utm.edu/departments/ed/cece/
   ducks.shtml

North American Hunting Retriever Association
http://www.nahra.org

Puddler—For Ducks Unlimited Greenwings
http://www.ducks.org/puddler/greenwings/
   home2.htm

U.S. Fish and Wildlife Service
http://www.fws.gov

Index